Theorem Appliqué: Book II

SUMMER SPLENDOR

by Patricia B. Campbell and Mimi Ayars

CHITRA PUBLICATIONS

Chitra Publications
2 Public Avenue
Montrose, Pennsylvania 18801

First printing: 1995

Campbell, Patricia B. (Patricia Bojan)
    Theorem applique.

  Contents: Bk. 1. Abundant harvest -- bk. 2.
Summer splendor.
   I. Applique--Patterns. 2. Wall hangings.
I. Ayars, Mimi. II. Abundant harvest.
III. Title.
TT779.C367 1994   746.44'50433   94-31563
ISBN 0-9622565-9-5 (v. 1)
ISBN 1-885588-03-8 (v. 2)

Editor: Janice P. Johnson
Design and Illustration: Kimberly L. Grace
Photography: Guy Cali Associates, Clarks Summit, PA
Black and white photography: Bradley Chrisenberry, Dallas, TX

Dedicated to our mentors
Olga Cheyunski, who envisioned Pat's becoming a star in the quilt world
and
Anna Janney DeArmond & John A. Munroe, who inspired Mimi's becoming an author.

In Appreciation
Thanks to the following people for their help in making "Summer Splendor."

Sally Ashbacher, Dallas, Texas	Embroiderer
Sharon Chambers, Mesquite, Texas	Stitcher
Jennie Boyes, Tulsa, Oklahoma	Stitcher
Joy Esau, Broken Arrow, Oklahoma	Stitcher
Michelle Jack, Garland, Texas	Quilter
Patricia M. Gabriel, Conover, North Carolina	Stitcher
Lee Patterson, Waco, Texas	Stitcher
Sue Troyan, Grapevine, Texas	Stitcher
Mary Warren, Tulsa, Oklahoma	Stitcher
Alice Wilhoit, Anna, Texas	Stitcher
Jeffrey Gutcheon, The American Classic Line	Background fabric
H.D. Wilbanks, Jr., Hobbs Bonded Fibers	Batting

"The late summer garden
has a tranquillity found
no other time of the year."
—William Longgood

INTRODUCTION

In the early 1800's theorem painting captivated girls at school and ladies at leisure. It became so popular it dethroned embroidery—the queen of feminine pursuits—and made her a lady-in-waiting. However, theorem painting reigned only a short time.

Now, in the late 1900's, it is experiencing a regal comeback in another form—not pigment but fabric, not brush but needle, not theorem painting but theorem appliqué. Designed in the spirit of antique theorem paintings, "Summer Splendor" is a princess of a wall hanging, pretty to look at and fun to do.

A girl of yesteryear had three goals in life: to be a wife, a mother and a lady. She prepared by attending a seminary (the name given to a girl's school in those days) where she learned reading, writing, ciphering (arithmetic), piano playing, dancing and painting. She practiced at home, where her mother was teacher and role model.

As an adult, her hands were constantly occupied because she took literally the saying, "idle hands are the devil's workshop." As a wife and mother, she began her domestic chores at sunup and continued beyond sundown with no microwave, breadmaking machine, takeout food, electricity or hot running water.

There was little time for leisure and a limited choice of ladylike activities for her "free" time. Theorem painting became popular because she enjoyed doing it and got encouragement from her family and community.

Even without instruction, a woman could create a still life composition and hang it in the parlor with pride. She accomplished this with theorems: a series of stencils, usually designed and cut by a professional artist. Using the stencils one at a time, in a specific order, she applied paint through the aperture of theorem #1. When the pigment dried, she repeated the process with theorem #2 and a different color, continuing with successive stencils and paints until the composition was completed. If a small mistake was made, she covered it up by painting in a butterfly or a bird.

Although the lifestyle of women who painted 150 years ago and the women who appliqué today is very different, they have one thing in common—a yearning to create beautiful things. You can find pleasure as great as your 19th century counterpart. Make a theorem appliqué wall quilt reminiscent of an antique theorem painting and hang it with pride in your "parlor."

Patricia B. Campbell has created theorem appliqué designs for "Summer Splendor." Mimi Ayars' concise instructions, together with photographs, will help you create a 52" x 52" wall quilt "to die for."

Although coordinated with *Theorem Appliqué: Book I, Abundant Harvest, Theorem Appliqué: Book II, Summer Splendor* contains all the information needed for making a wall quilt that reflects the theme and composition of an old theorem painting. Two more theorem appliqué books will follow. Look for them in quilt shops and book stores.

PREPARATION

MATERIALS

- 2 1/2 yards 45" background fabric:100% cotton, off-white
- 3 1/4 yards 45" backing fabric: 100% cotton
- 1/2 yard 45" binding fabric: 100% cotton, blue
- Appliqué design fabrics: 100% cotton, variety
- 1 1/2 yards 54" batting: lightweight
- 1 package (15" x 3 yds.) interfacing: inexpensive, lightweight, nonwoven, nonfusible
- Appliqué thread: machine embroidery, variety of colors to match fabrics
- Quilting thread: off-white
- Embroidery floss: dark olive green and black-brown
- Template plastic: clear

Use 100% cotton fabric throughout the wall quilt. An off-white background, plain or tone-on-tone, mimics the velvet background of old theorem paintings. Purchase high quality, evenly woven fabric; it will hang well. Gutcheon's The American Classic Line™ was used for "Summer Splendor." A wide array of design fabrics permits realistic treatment of flowers, fruits, bowls, baskets and butterflies. Cotton is easier to needleturn than blends, silk or rayon. The cotton backing can be any shade or pattern. For the binding, choose one of the blue fabrics you will use in your design; cut the binding strips before the appliqué pieces.

The package of inexpensive interfacing is for the master patterns. You need to see through it for tracing ease. Because the thread must match the appliqué, a variety of fabrics means a variety of threads. Machine embroidery thread hides well because it is fine. Clear plastic is essential for making the templates and for placing the templates on the design fabric.

TOOLS

- Pencils: silver, white, mechanical
- Pen: thin line, permanent black
- Scissors, 2 pairs: sharp for fabric, craft for templates
- Pins: sashiko, sequin and quilting
- Needles: #10 or #12 betweens
- Sandpaper board
- Cardboard: 16" square
- Ruler
- Rotary cutter and mat
- Sewing machine

The pen is used to draw the master patterns on the interfacing. Use a pen or a pencil to draw the templates. A sandpaper board under the fabric keeps it from slipping while marking the design pieces. Good light and a comfortable chair mean prettier stitches and delayed fatigue.

CUTTING FABRIC BLOCKS, BORDERS AND BINDING

The overall measurements for the wall quilt are 52" x 52". The blocks will finish to 16" x 16" and the borders to 10" x 52". The following illustration is your cutting guide. Be sure the pieces are cut square and on grain.

	17"	17"	56"	
17"	Block	Block	Border	11"
			Border	11"
17"	Block	Block	Border	11"
	Leftover		Border	11"

As you cut each piece, tag it with a scrap of paper in the upper right hand corner. You will then know which is the right side and you will have the grain of the pieces going in the same direction. Notice the position of the tags below.

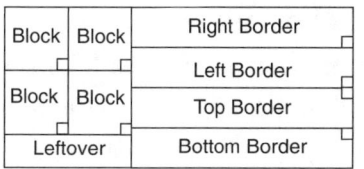

Cut from the background fabric:
- Four 17" squares for the blocks, 16" finished.
- Four 11" x 56" rectangles for the borders, 10" x 52" finished.

Cut crosswise from the blue binding fabric:
- Five strips 1 1/4" wide, to make 216".

Cut the strips on the straight of grain and sew them right sides together, end to end, with 1/4" bias seams. Finger press the seams open without stretching them.

MASTER PATTERNS

Cut from the interfacing:
- Four 15" squares for the blocks.
- Four 7 1/2" x 24" rectangles for the borders.

The fabric squares are bigger than the interfacing squares, but the designs fit within this space.

In this book, each block pattern is divided into four parts, each part on a separate page. Trace the quadrants of Block 1 onto a square of interfacing with a permanent black pen. The broken lines and center point help you align the parts; include them on the master pattern. Do this for the other three blocks.

The border pattern is shown in sections, one section per page. Although the pattern must be traced on all four fabric borders, only one master is needed because of the repeat. Trace the sections, abutting one section to the next. Mark the broken lines and the center point on the master pattern as shown below. The other three pieces of interfacing will be used later.

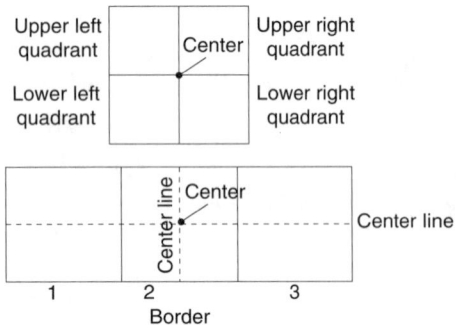

MARKING PATTERNS ON FABRIC

Find the center of Block 1 by folding the fabric square in half one way and then in half the other way. Pinch where the folds come together. Unfold and lightly mark with pencil on the wrong side where the folds cross as shown in the diagram.

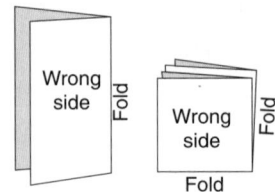

Push a pin through the center from the right side of the block into the center of the pattern held beneath it. Square up the two. Draw the pattern on the fabric block, keeping the pencil lines 1/4" inside the master pattern lines so there is less chance of having to remove pencil marks when the stitching is completed. Mark the remaining blocks the same way.

To find the center of a border piece, fold the rectangle in half lengthwise, right sides together. Mark lightly with pencil along the fold. Unfold and fold in half widthwise. Mark lightly where the vertical crease crosses the horizontal pencil lines. This is the center. Draw the pattern on the fabric, staying 1/4" inside the master pattern lines. Use an "X" to indicate the placement of circles. Repeat these steps with the three remaining border pieces.

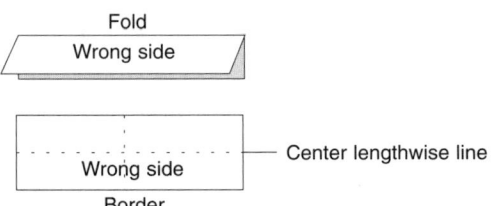

MAKING TEMPLATES

Using the Block 1 master pattern, draw templates of the appliqué pieces on clear plastic template material. Cut them out carefully.

After cutting the circle templates, check for little peaks on the edge. If you find any, smooth them off with an emery board. Perfect circle templates make perfect circle design pieces.

Lay the templates for Block 1 in their proper place on the master pattern. If you are concerned about their getting out of place, number the spaces on the master pattern and their corresponding templates with a permanent black pen. Make templates for the other blocks and border.

MARKING AND CUTTING DESIGN PIECES

Place your design fabric right side up on a sandpaper board to prevent slippage while marking. Place a template from the master pattern of Block 1 on your design fabric. Use the bias as much as possible to reduce fraying and to make needle-turning easier. Trace around the template with a sharp pencil held so that the top tilts slightly outward. This permits you to get close to the template. The line is your stitching line, not your cutting line. Cut the pieces out, adding only 1/8" seam allowance. The slim amount of fabric to turn under helps you appliqué well.

Pin the design pieces on the master pattern as you cut them. After all the pieces have been pinned for the first block, view the arrangement. If any piece doesn't please you, replace it. Store the used templates in a plastic bag identified "Block 1." Repeat these steps with the other blocks.

You have traced the master pattern for the border on only one rectangle of interfacing because it is a repeat, but you have drawn the pattern on all four fabric rectangles. Cut four appliqué pieces for each template. Pin one set of design pieces on the master pattern and pin the other sets in their approximate positions on the other interfacing rectangles ready for later placement on border pieces.

When all the pieces for "Summer Splendor" have been pinned, arrange the interfacing pieces as the blocks and border will be assembled. Look at the complete composition. If you like the distribution of color and pattern, you are ready to stitch.

STITCHING

A fun aspect of appliqué is that the stitcher can move from one part of the composition to another as long as the underneath piece is stitched first. Starting with a block, lay an "underneath" design piece in its proper place. The 1/8" seam allowance generally makes it unnecessary to clip. Begin stitching on a gentle curve, never at a point.

Knot a 15" to 18" piece of thread that matches the design piece. Bring the thread up from the back of the design fabric through the pencil line. With the tip of the needle about 3/4" ahead of where the thread comes up, sweep the needle toward you, turning the seam allowance under. This is needle-turning.

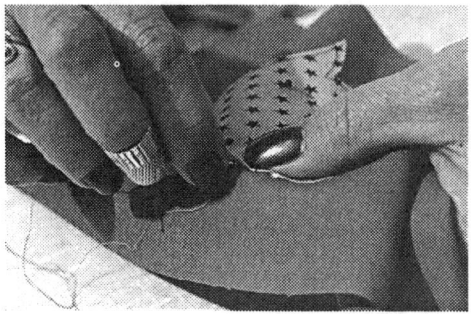

Put your needle point into the background fabric, directly adjacent to where your needle emerged on the marked line and slightly under the fold of the design fabric. Pick up two or three threads and come up into the design fabric on the marked line (which is now the fold) about 1/16" from the last stitch. The picking up of the threads and the emergence into the fold are one motion.

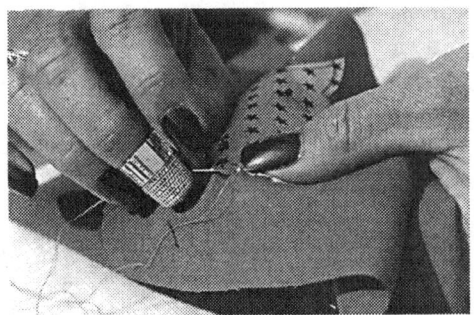

Take several stitches and needleturn. Continue stitching the pieces in place. To minimize fatigue, make sure you position your hands so that your thumbs face each other, as shown in the photos.

When your thread is too short to continue, put your needle through to the back of the background fabric, just inside the edge of the design piece. Take a little "bite" of the background fabric with your needle as shown. Repeat with a second "bite."

Bury the thread by passing the needle between the two layers away from the edge. Snip the thread close to the background fabric. Thread the needle, make a knot and start stitching again with the needle coming up at the pencil line, very close to the last stitch. The new knot will be hidden in the fold. Continue stitching as before.

POINTS

Stitch to the marked point. Take a stitch on top of the last stitch to secure it. Remove your thimble and set your threaded needle in the background fabric, out of the way. Turn the block as if you were going to start stitching down the other side. Clip off any little bit of fabric from the seam allowance of the first side that pokes out.

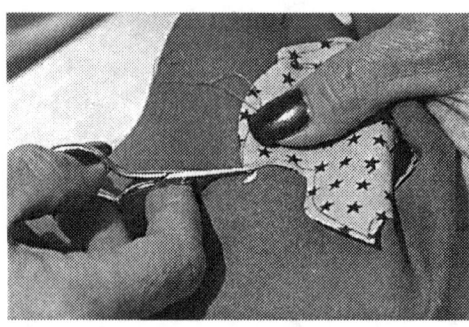

Hold the stitch at the point and the thread firmly under your thumbnail. With a quilter's pin grasped about 1/2" up from the point and braced from behind with your middle finger, sweep the seam allowance under from right to left, all the time holding the point tightly with your thumbnail, lifting it only when you sweep the fabric under. Then sweep left to right. If you don't like the result, pull the seam allowance out with your needle and try again, sweeping right to left and then left to right.

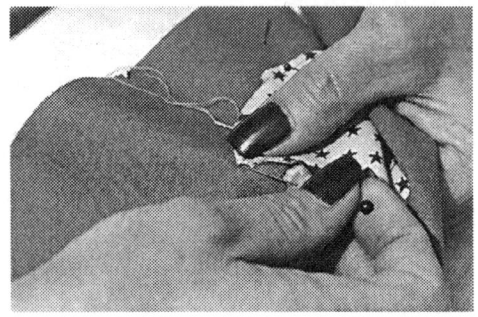

Still holding the point tightly with your thumbnail, take a 1/16" stitch out from the point into the background fabric. Unlike your other stitches that you've been trying to hide, you want this one to show. The extra stitch elongates the point, giving the illusion that the tip is more pointed than it really is. Continue stitching down the other side.

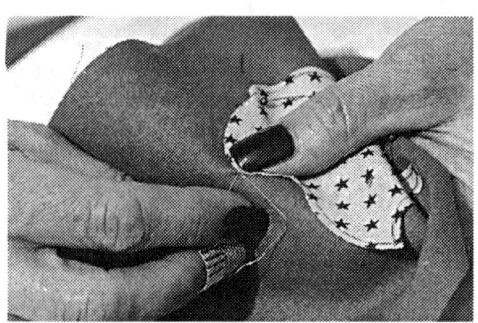

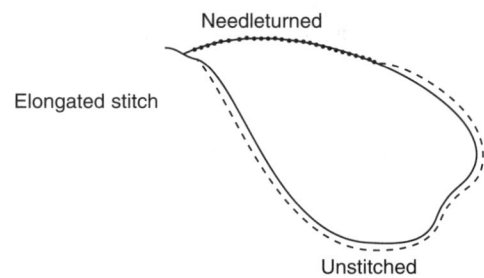

CIRCLES

There is no need to clip the seam allowance. Using a sequin pin on the underside to hold the circle in place, needleturn only enough to take one stitch. Take that one stitch, turn the circle, needleturn, then take another stitch. Needleturning a slim seam allowance, taking only one stitch, and turning the circle create a smooth round circle.

EMBROIDERY

Theorem artists painted the tendrils and stems freehand after the stenciling was completed. To reflect this delicate painting, theorem appliqué artists embroider the tendrils and stems after the appliqué is completed. Choose the stitch and colors you prefer. The backstitch was used in "Summer Splendor" with dark olive green for the tendrils and black-brown for the stems.

FINISHING

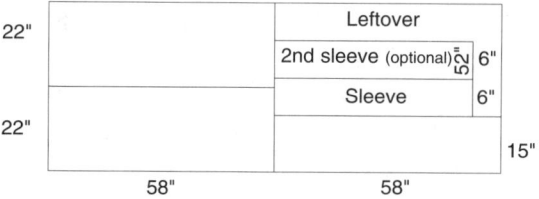

ASSEMBLING

Find the center of your 16" cardboard square by drawing diagonal lines from corner to corner. The intersection is the center. Make a tiny hole at that point with the tip of your scissors. Pass a pin through the hole of the template into the center of the wrong side of the marked fabric block. Square the two. Draw with pencil around the cardboard. These are your sewing lines. Mark the other blocks in the same way.

Sew the blocks together. Trim the seams to 1/4" and press gently.

You have made pencil marks on the wrong side of the border pieces along the lengthwise center line. Mark the sewing lines by measuring 5" out on each side of this line.

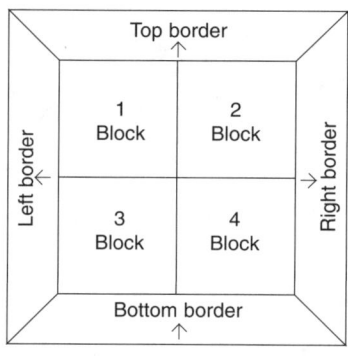

Note the direction of the arrows for positioning the border pieces. Sew the border pieces to the assembled blocks, matching centers. Stop sewing within 1/4" of each end. Trim the seam to 1/4", but do not cut off the leftover fabric at each end. Miter the corners. Now trim away the excess fabric. Finger press.

With a dry iron, press the top gently on the wrong side. Trim the outside edge of the borders leaving a 1/4" seam allowance.

QUILTING

Cut from the backing fabric:
• Two pieces 22" x 58".
• One piece 15" x 58".

Sew these using 1/4" seams, with the narrow piece in the middle. Press. The backing will be longer and wider than the top.

Baste the top, batting and backing together, leaving the surplus evenly distributed on all sides. Hobbs wool batting was used for "Summer Splendor." Turn the backing over to the front temporarily, basting with safety pins, to protect the edges while you quilt.

Shadow quilt, then echo quilt twice the flowers, fruits, bowls, baskets and butterflies. Do simple line quilting in the background that does not detract from the design.

SLEEVE

Wall quilts are made for hanging so you'll need a sleeve.

Cut from the backing fabric (not the background fabric): One or two 9" x 52" rectangle.

Sew double 1/4" seams at each 9" end. On the right side measure 1 1/2" in from one of the 52" sides. Fold along this line, wrong sides together. Machine baste a 1/2" tuck along the fold. With the tuck on the outside, fold the strip in half lengthwise, keeping the raw edges even. Pin, then sew the sleeve (tuck toward you) to the top of the quilt with a 1/8" seam. Pin and stitch the lower edge of the sleeve by hand. Pull out the basting. Some quiltmakers like to put a sleeve at the bottom also. An inserted batten (a piece of wood or plastic) helps it hang well because of the additional weight. There is enough fabric to make a second sleeve, if you wish.

BINDING

To keep the edges of the quilt straight, not wavy, baste close to the edges of the quilt before sewing on the binding. Start sewing about 2" down from one corner, leaving a 2" tail of binding free. Bind the quilt, using any method you like, but be sure the corners are square. To finish the binding, stop sewing a few inches from where you began. Turn the first end back at a 45° angle and sew the last end straight down. Trim.

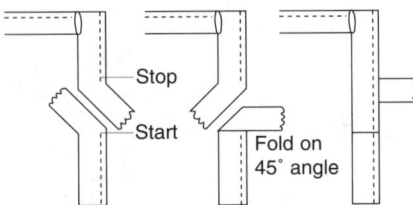

Turn the binding to the back, fold under 1/4", pin, and stitch by hand. Tack the corners and the joining ends.

DOCUMENTATION

Make a label, indicating the name "Summer Splendor" (or a name of your choice), the date, your name, and any other information you think your heirs might like to know. Sew the label onto the back. Hang your beautiful quilt with pride. Take a photo for your scrapbook. Tell your friends about theorem painting and theorem appliqué.

Book III will follow soon. Look for it!

If you have questions or want information about workshops, contact:

PATRICIA B. CAMPBELL
9794 Forest Lane
Suite 900
Dallas, Texas 75243
Voice or FAX 214-994-0977

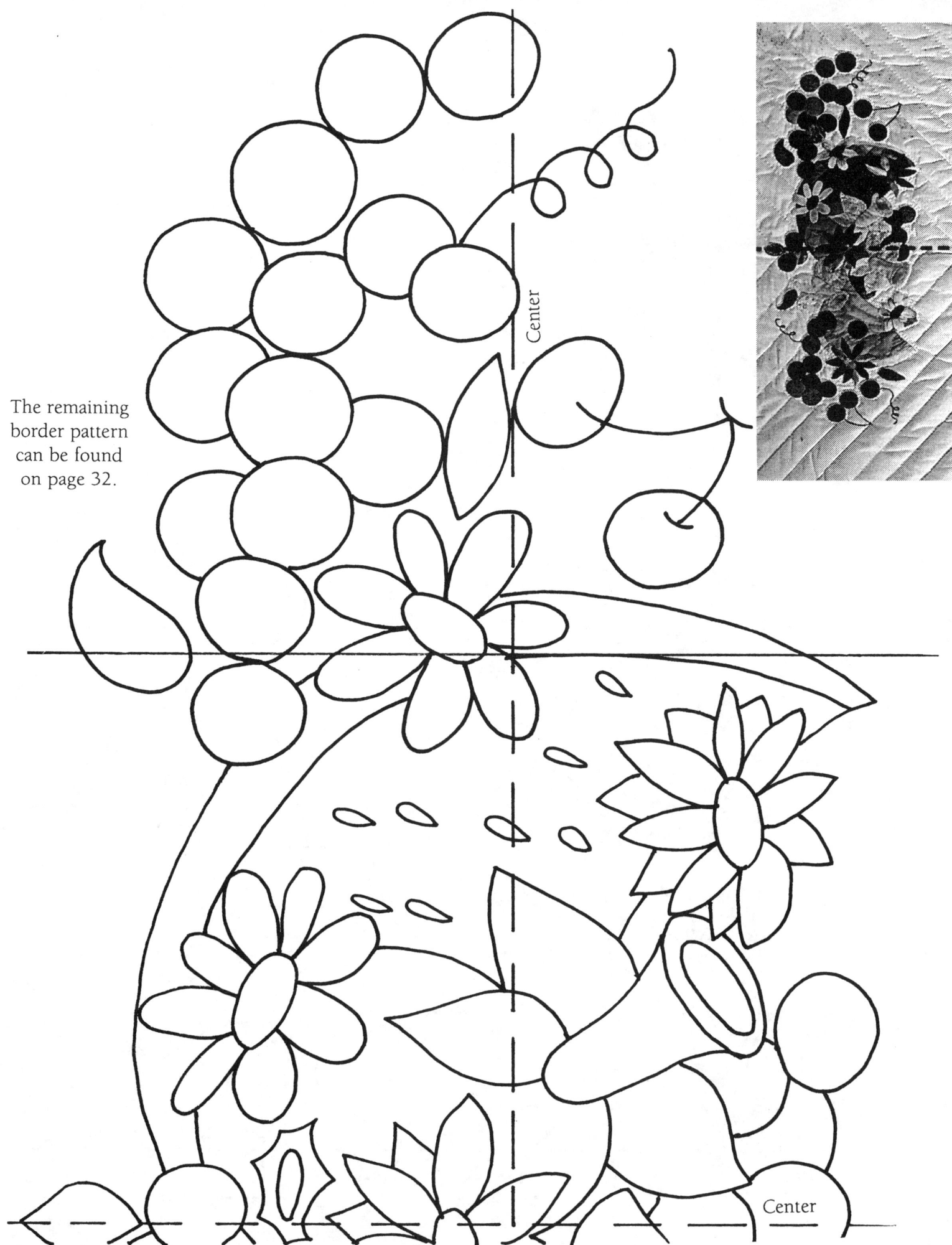

The remaining border pattern can be found on page 32.

Center

Center

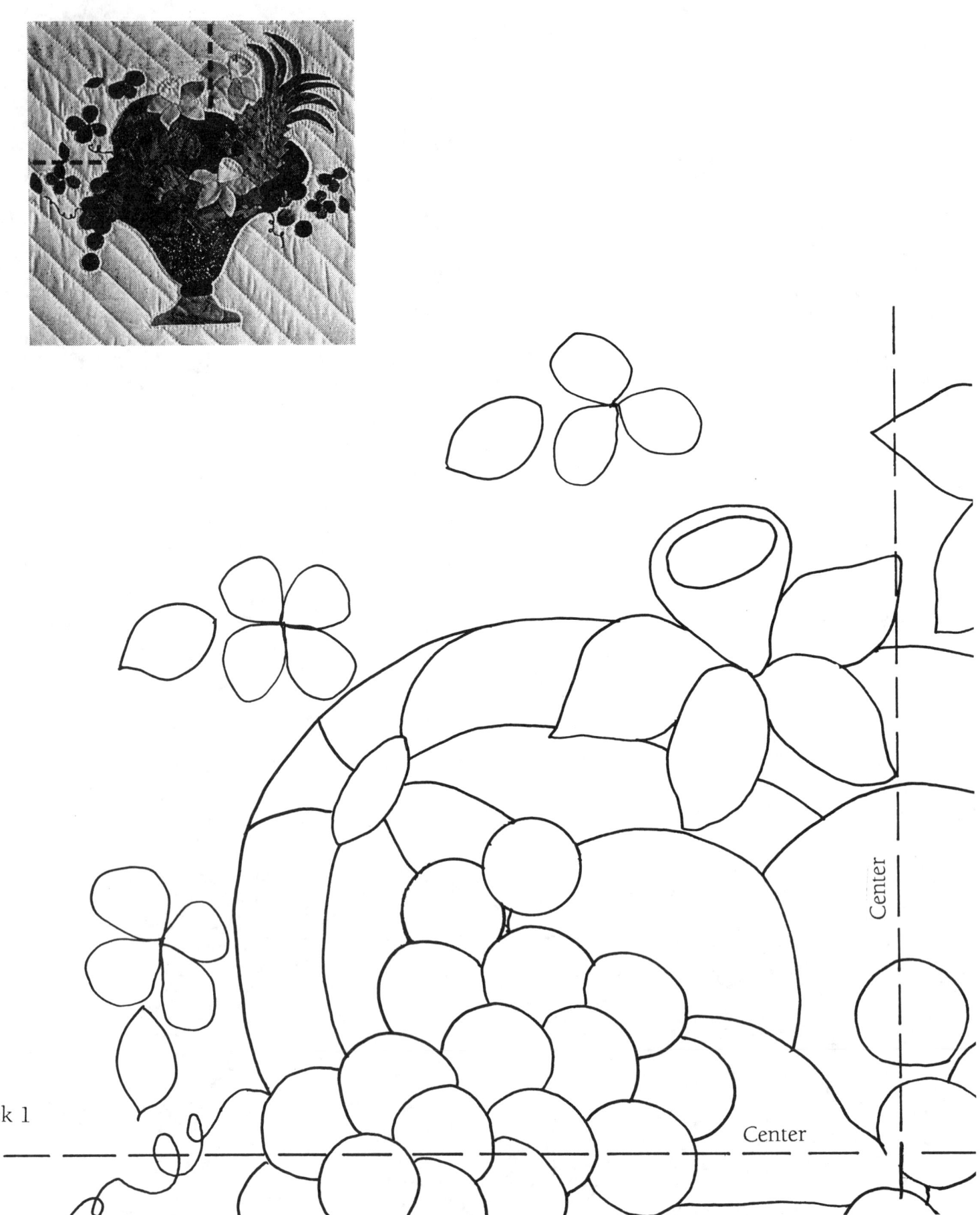

Block 1

Center

Center

Center

Center

Block 1

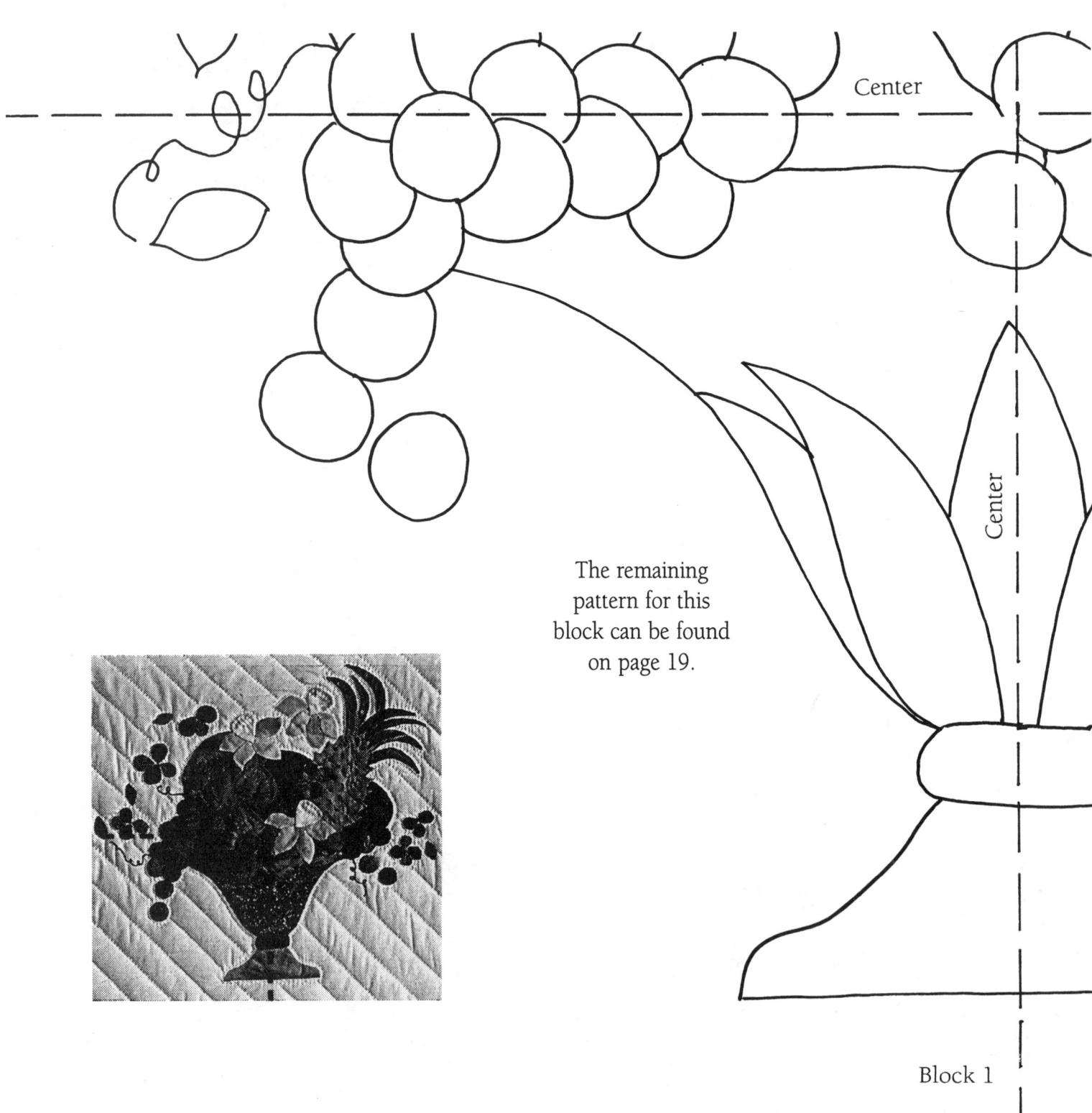

Center

Center

The remaining
pattern for this
block can be found
on page 19.

Block 1

Theorem Appliqué: Summer Splendor

Theorem Appliqué: Summer Splendor

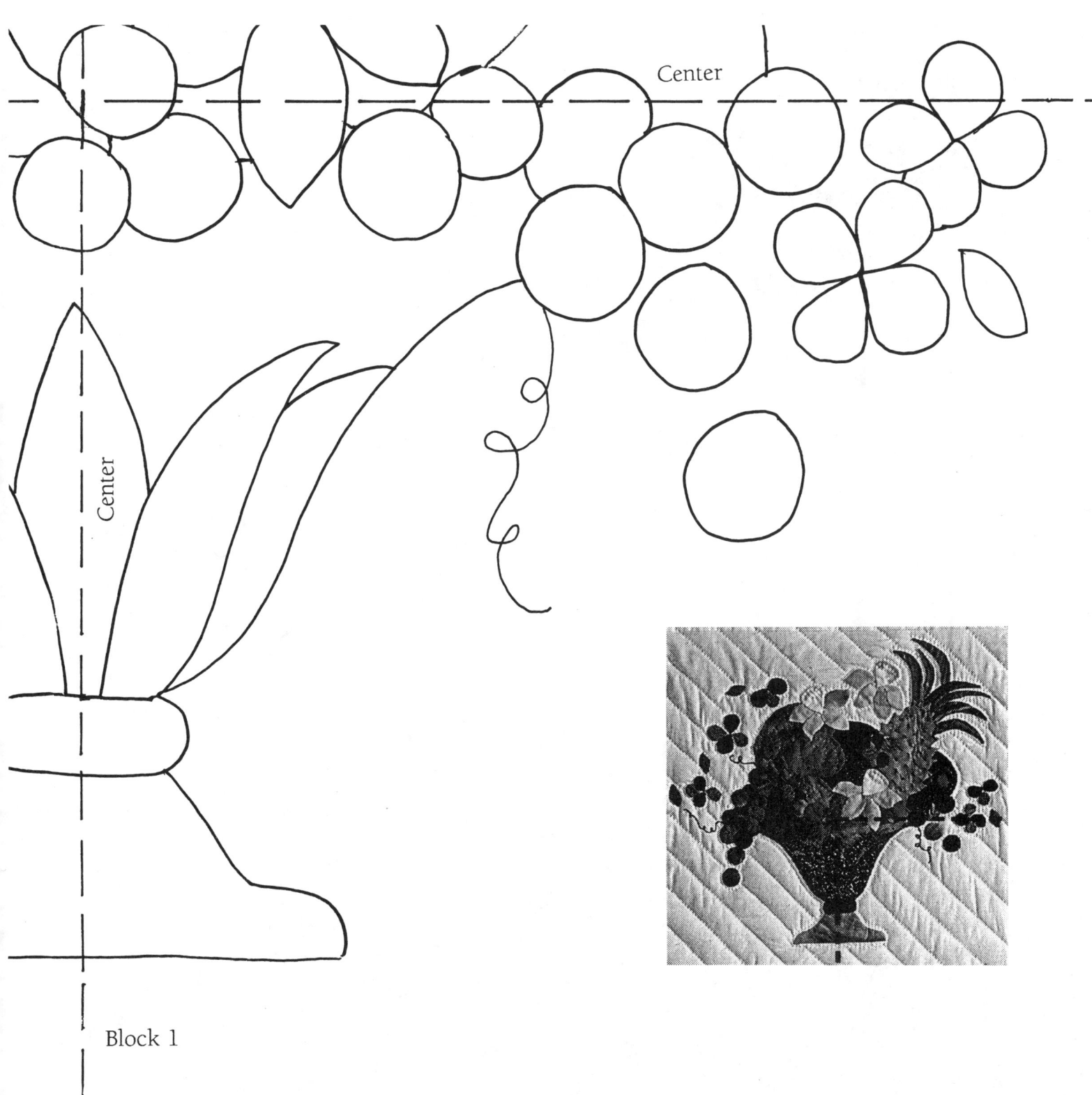

Center

Center

Block 1

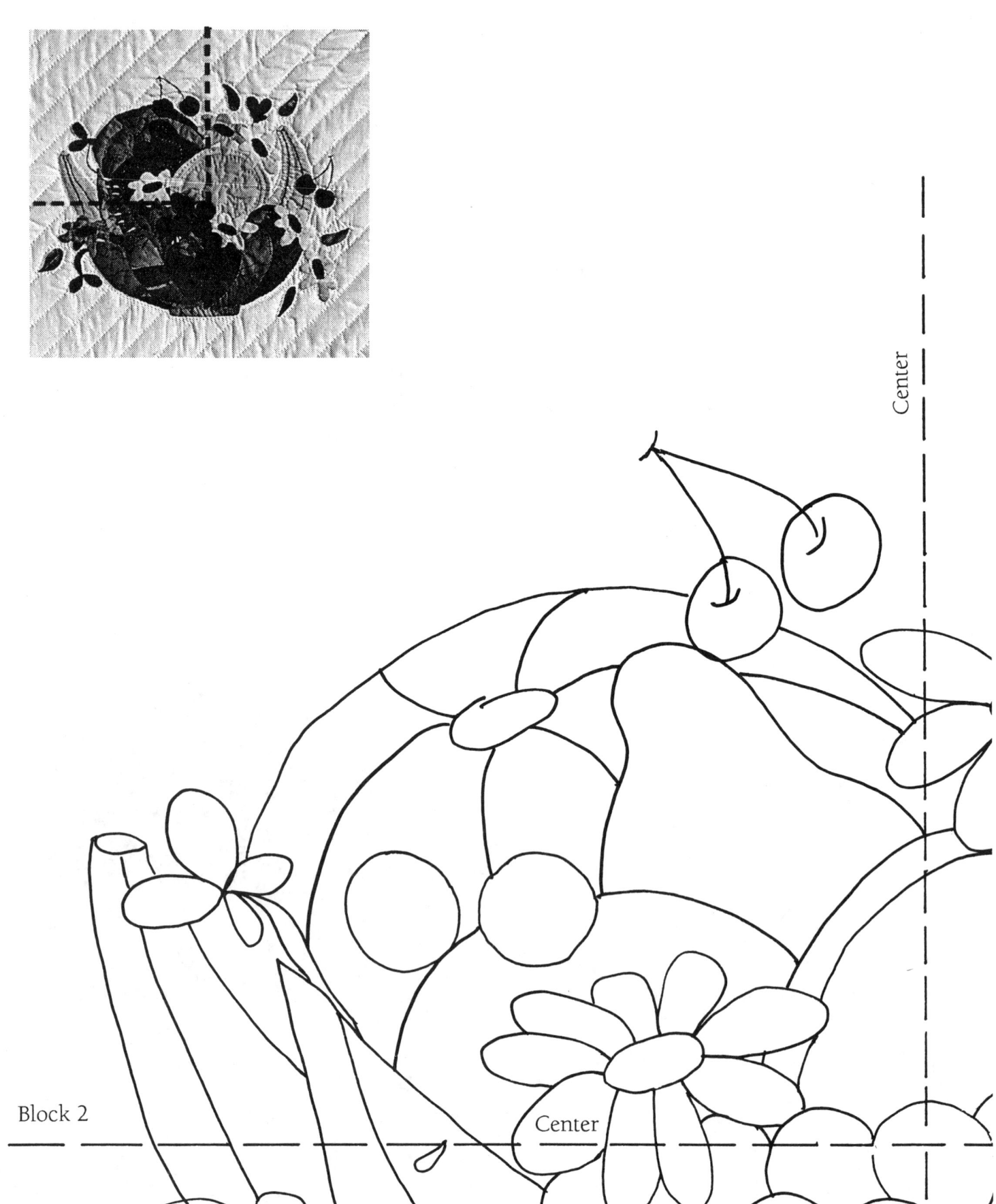

Center

Block 2

Center

Center

Center

Block 2

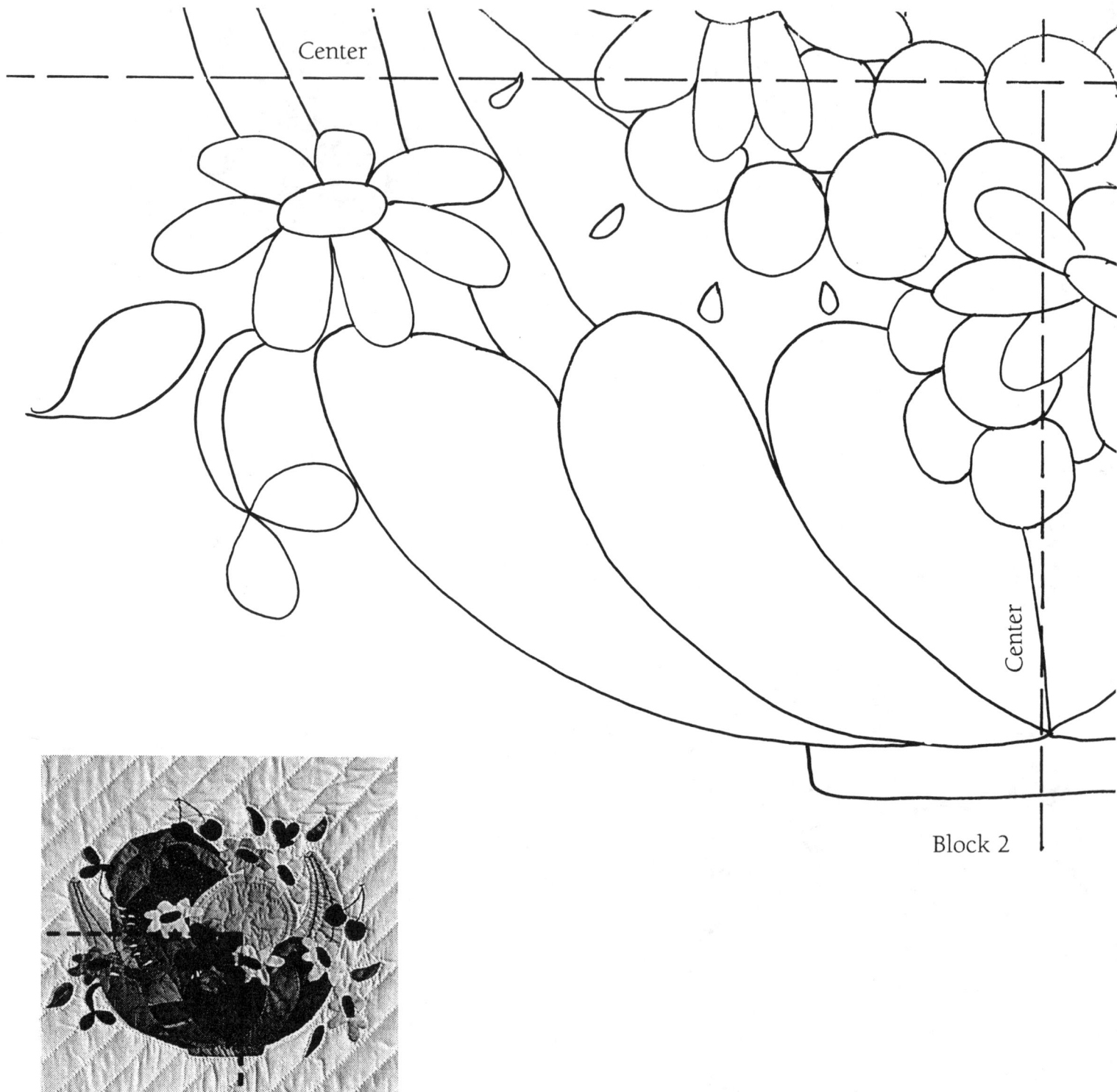

Center

Center

Block 2

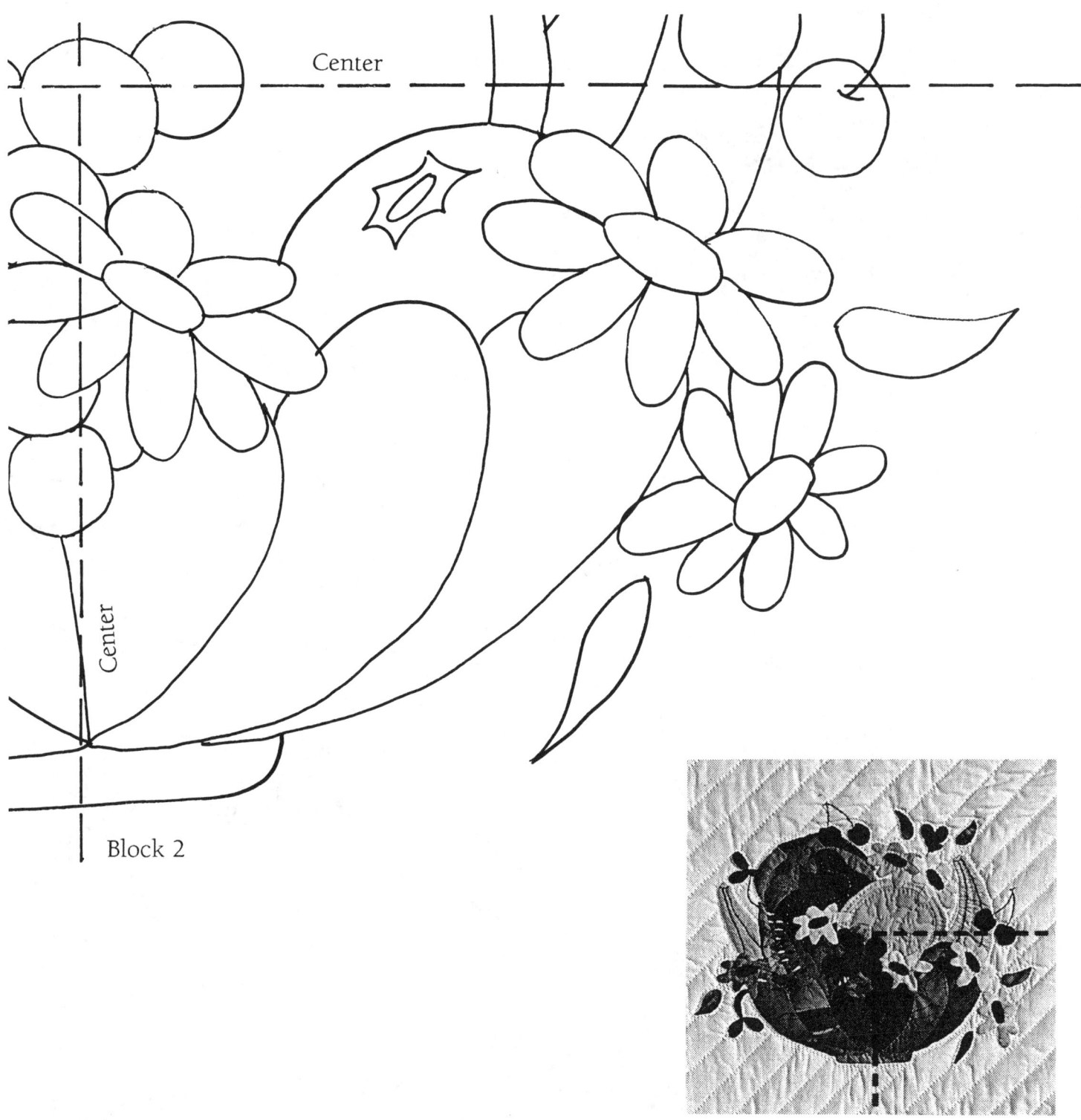

Center

Center

Block 2

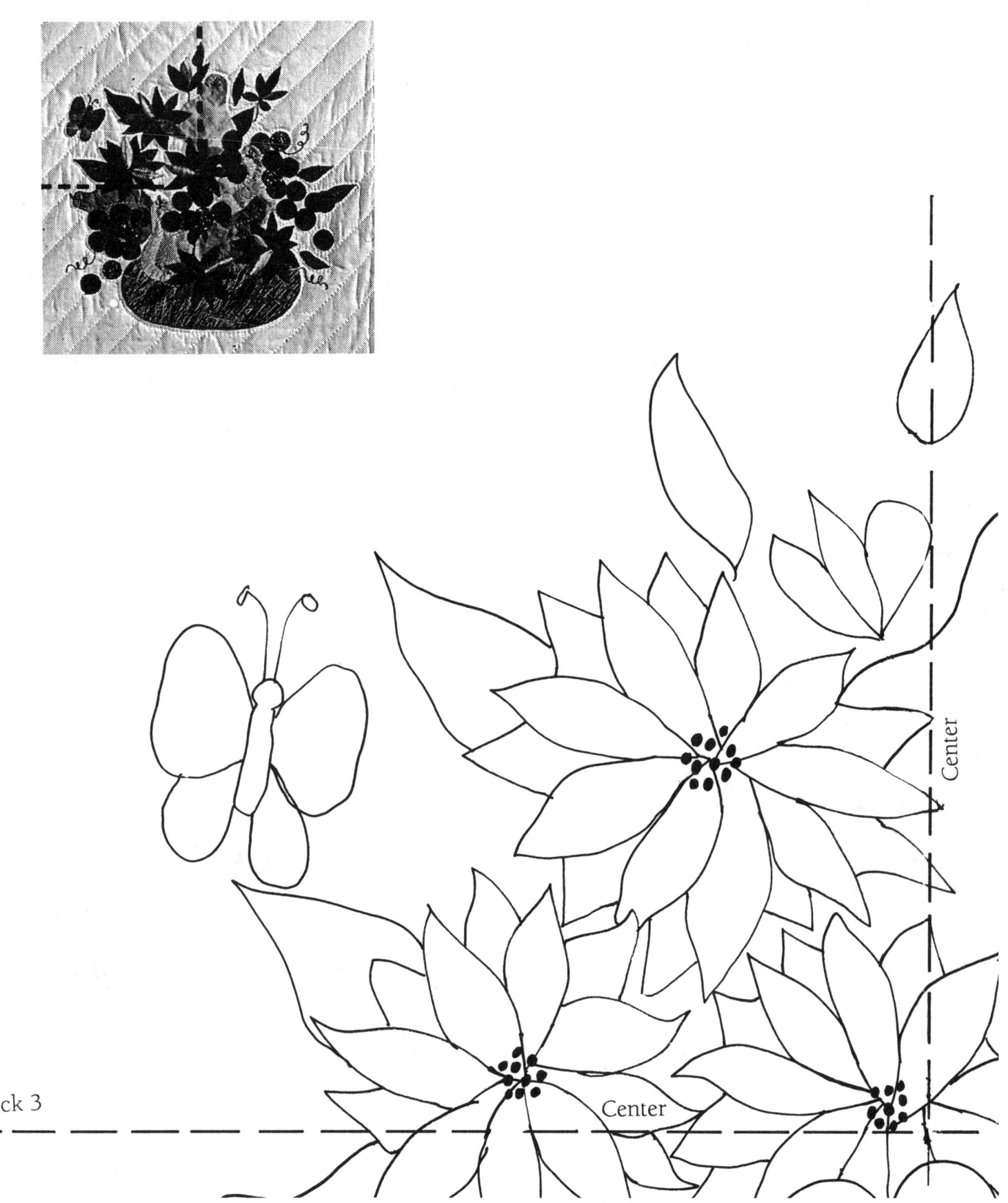

Block 3

Center

Center

Theorem Appliqué: Summer Splendor

Center

Center

Block 3

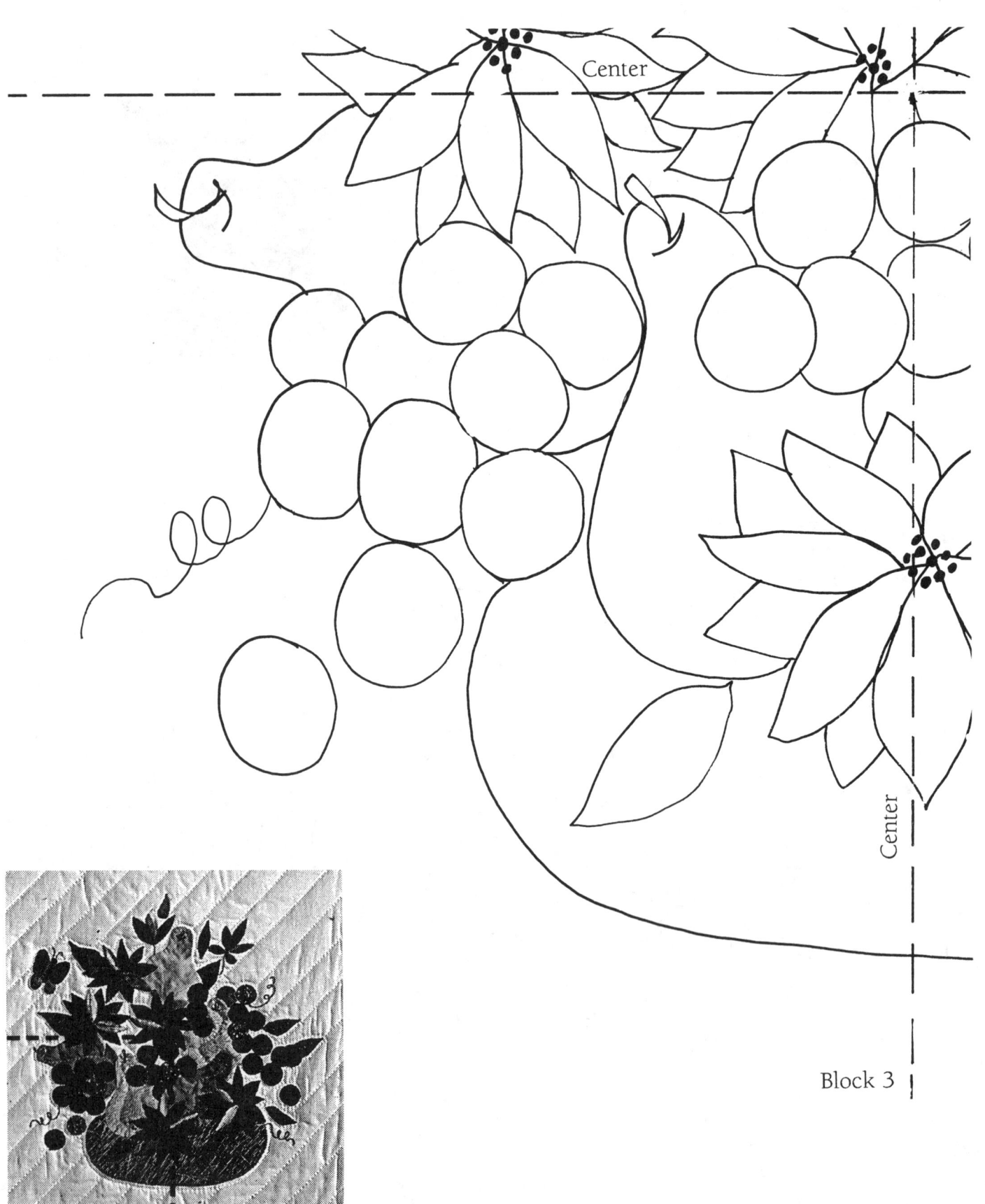

Center

Center

Block 3

Theorem Appliqué: Summer Splendor

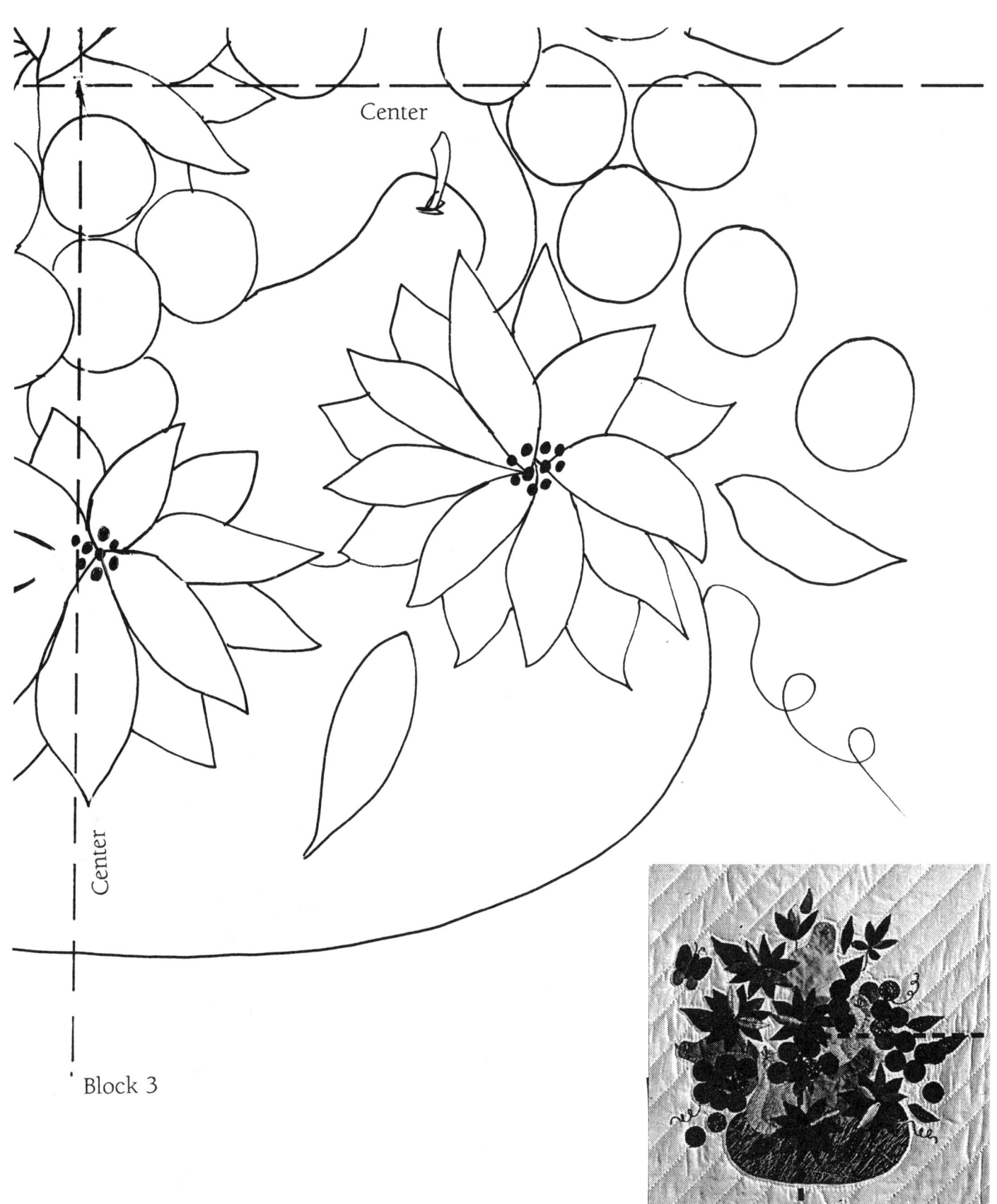

Center

Center

Block 3

Block 4

Center

Center

Theorem Appliqué: Summer Splendor

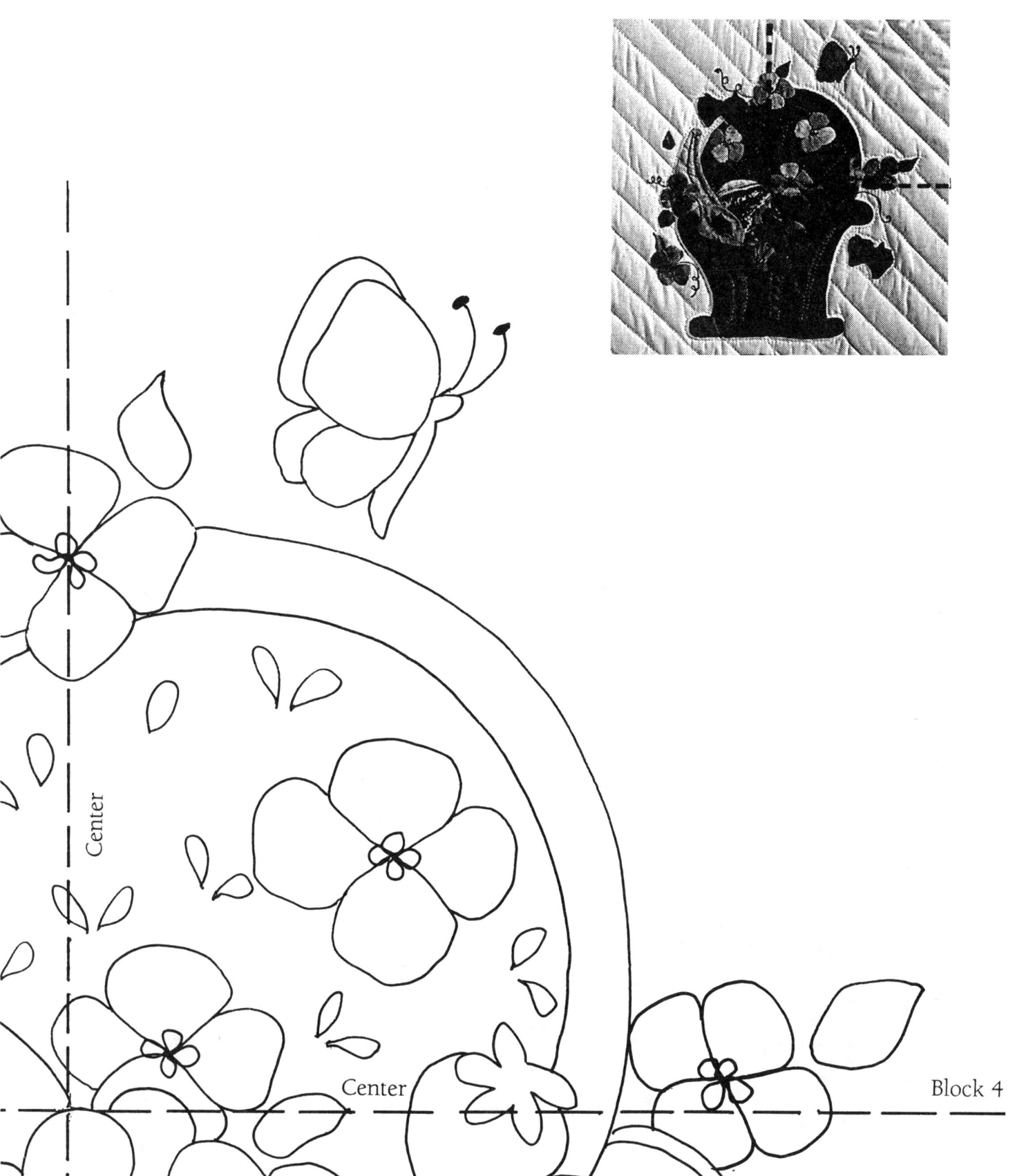

Center

Center

Block 4

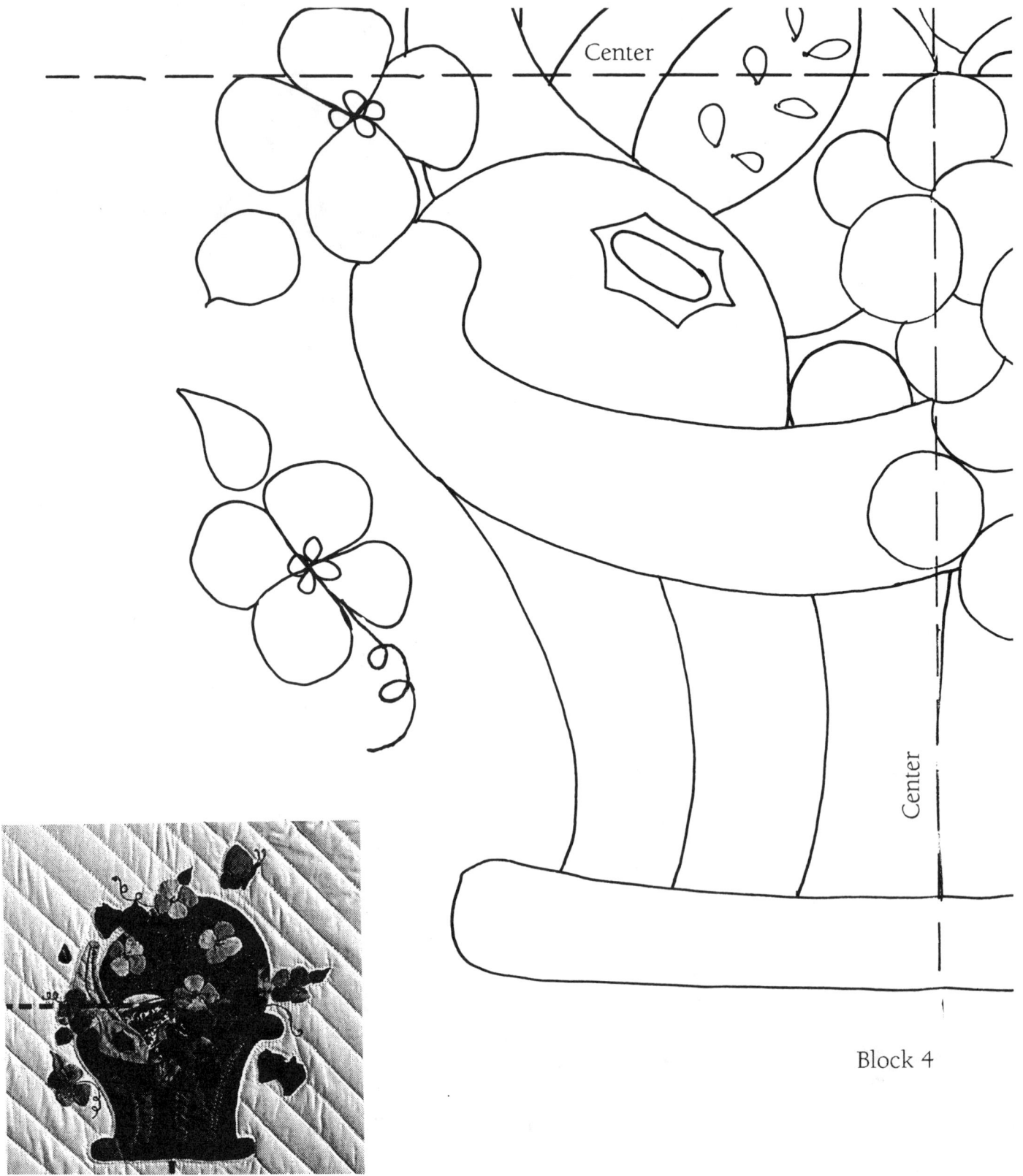

Center

Center

Block 4

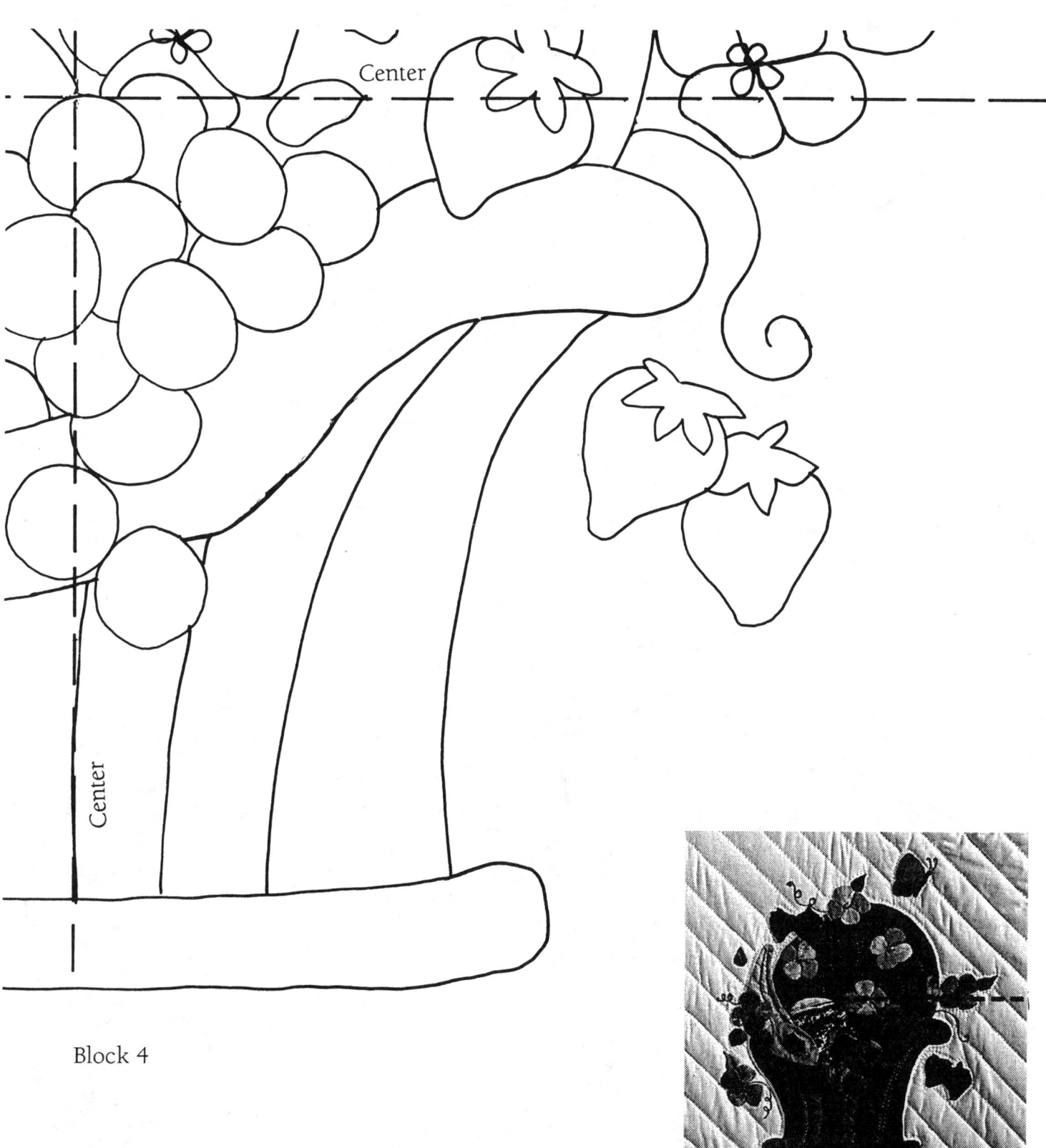

Center

Center

Block 4

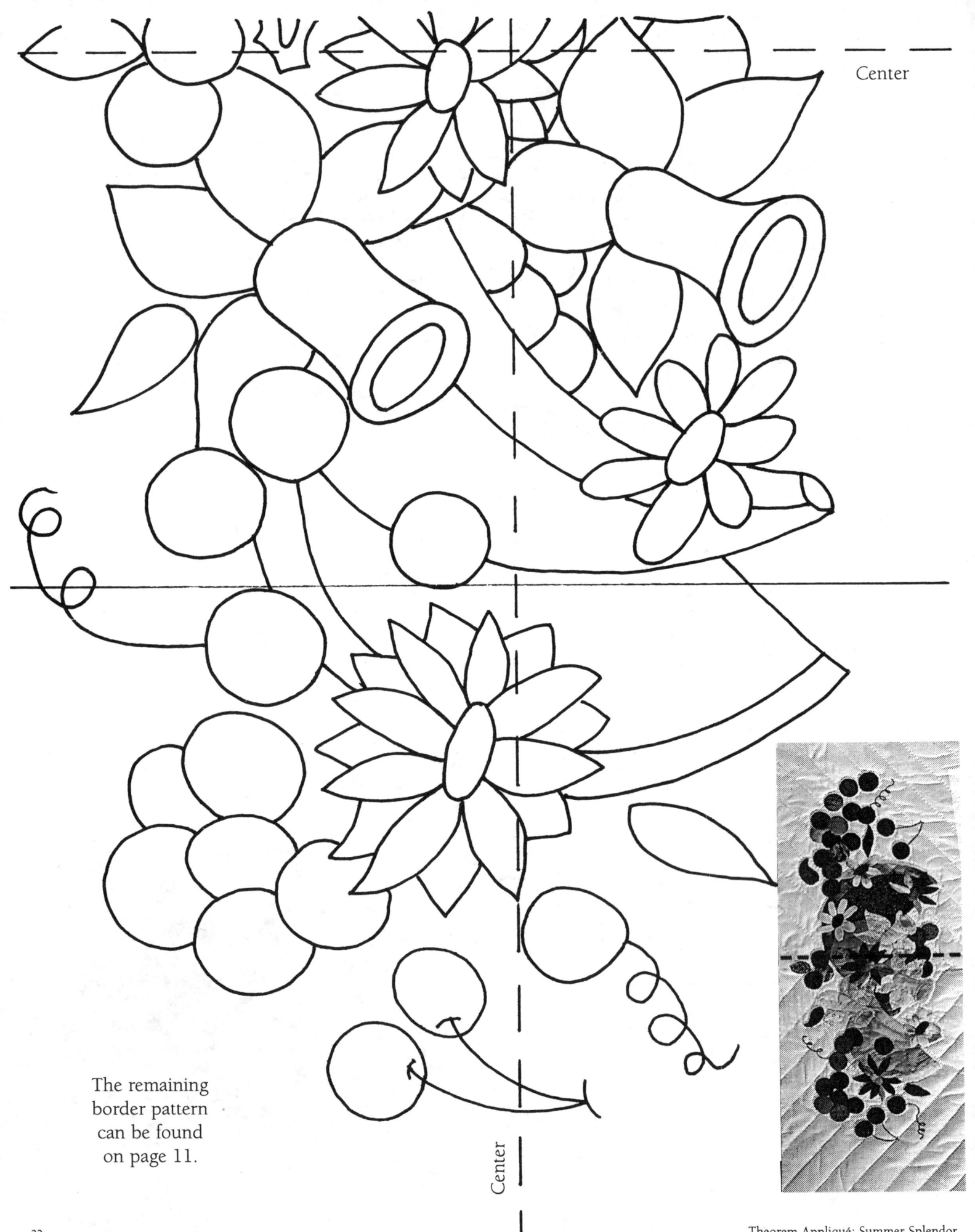

Center

The remaining
border pattern
can be found
on page 11.

Center

Theorem Appliqué: Summer Splendor